HOW TO MAKE FRIENDS

A PRACTICAL, REALISTIC GUIDE TO BUILDING BETTER SOCIAL SKILLS, MEANINGFUL RELATIONSHIPS & CONNECTING WITH PEOPLE

DARCY CARTER

RITUALS OF THE
RICH & FAMOUS

Free Success Tips, Strategies, and Habits of the Rich & Famous.

For new strategies every week on how to be more productive, confident, and happy.

JOIN SUCCESSFUL SUBSCRIBERS!

Simply scan the QR code to join.

CONTENTS

INTRODUCTION

Let's get real here. Do you ever struggle in social situations? Are you ever lost for words? Does it feel like you are lacking certain social skills? If any of this applies to you then keep on reading. I know how it feels. You're at a party and everyone is having a great time. It's like they all know each other. But you're all quiet, stuck inside your head and you just don't know what to say. Or maybe recently you met someone whom you admired but you didn't connect as well as you wanted to. It feels like something is holding you back. You go home frustrated, lonely, and fed up. For years this goes on and before you know it all your old friends are settled down. Meanwhile, you're looking for something to watch on Netflix. Alone. Worse, you're watching a rerun of some average series. But really you want to be with someone you enjoy being around. Someone to talk to. A best friend. Maybe you want a whole new set of friends to go out with. Or maybe you're just bored with life and need some sparkle added to it.

I understand you because I have experienced all of those feelings. Yes, I know, it sucks! But there is light at the end of the tunnel. Even if you lack friends, have social anxiety, awkwardness, or live in a quiet area. There is hope for you. Believe me, I know what it takes. I came from living in my parent's front room in an isolated village which was in the middle of nowhere. Coming out of a bad breakup at that time, I had no social skills, awkwardness, and not many friends. Actually, the closest friends I had were a two-hour drive to some lame city and they weren't exactly doing anything fun. Nights out with them would usually be spent getting wasted in some trashy place. This wasn't for me, and I felt lost. Deep down I knew I wanted friends who inspired me, who did cool things, and who were there for me.

Fast forward a few years to the whole pandemic thing. I was alone and frustrated by the lockdowns. As we all know socializing wasn't possible and for someone who loves socializing, it had started to make me depressed. Life felt stale and I needed an escape. I scrolled through Google and looked at all the countries in the world with the least restrictions. Argentina stood out to me. Wow, it seemed so exotic! So far away and way out of my comfort zone. This was a good sign that it would help me to grow as a person. So, with my suitcase in hand, I boarded the two fifteen-hour flights and arrived in South America knowing no one or any of the local languages. What started as a random spontaneous trip turned into extended periods of time spent in Argentina and Brazil. From the start, I knew nobody. But in the end, I had amazing friends from diverse backgrounds. All because I went out there and did what I will outline in this book.

Nowadays I have friends all over the world because I have figured out how to time and time again move somewhere new and connect with my kind of people. For me, that's motivated and interesting people who are doing cool things in their free time. They are friends who inspire me, who I learn from, who I trust, and who I can confide in. Friends I am proud to call my friend. Nowadays my social life is diverse and never run out of things to do or people to share experiences with. It is amazing to think of where it came from and how it is now.

In this book, I will share with you how that was possible for me and how you can do it too. Again, let me tell you that I have moved to places around the world knowing no one. Literally, I turned up in new cities with zero friends. But multiple times I have left there with a whole new social circle of cool people. Anytime I go back I can pick up where I left off. How? Because I followed the system outlined in this book. From trial and error, I have found that yes, this stuff works. Not only for myself but I have seen others do it. All of that information is inside this book for you to learn from and use. It's not complicated, and it is possible for everyone regardless of their circumstances.

What I offer is a system. Wait a system? I know what you're thinking. I'm not a robot. Yes and neither am I! Please don't get confused with the terminology here. When I say system it's more of a collection of habits, actions, and accountability. This is what will turn your life from boring to booming. Maybe you want to meet a new best friend to share your life with. Or maybe you want a whole new social circle. Those things can happen. But I promise you they won't just appear out of thin air. Following the system, I and the accountability for that happening are on you. After all, it is your life.

Now is the time for you to have a new lease on life. The world is open again! Start creating a life with a buzzing social calendar, amazing friends, and always something interesting to do. No more lonely, boring nights on the sofa looking for the next series. Such a life will energize you to wake up in the morning knowing that many adventures are ahead of you. Do the work in this book and good things will keep snowballing into your life. Because of people. Think about it. Anything good in your life or your achievements likely came because of a person. Naturally, having more quality people in your life will enhance the quality of your life.

Growth might feel weird, challenging, and difficult. But progress is part of that. There is light at the end of the tunnel. Now don't see this as a hard thing to do. Remember this will be a fun journey for the most part so embrace the ride. You're not getting younger. People won't just magically appear on your doorstep. It's on you to go out there and meet people. It will require some work, but I promise you it will be worth it. Now there is little more time to waste. Let's go!

YOUR SOCIAL LIFE

Proven research has concluded that the average human being can establish a social network of up to one hundred and fifty people. (Dunbar, 2010) Within that, there are limits to the depth and degree of the relationships. Naturally, we cannot have deep connections with all of the one hundred and fifty people. Realistically we could have about fifty acquaintances which then narrows down to smaller circles of closer friends. Over the course of our lifetimes, we will evolve and change those circles which is the natural progression of life. People grow up, get married, have kids, move on, and so on.

Now before you go any further with reading this book, I want you to ask yourself some real questions. What kind of friends do you want? How do you want your social life to look? Because if you want real results, then you need to know what to aim for. Maybe you are dissatisfied and lonely. Maybe you want to meet a new group of friends to go out with. Maybe your best friend just got into a relationship, and you are looking for someone to fill their gap. Maybe you want someone to hang out with and have deep conversations with. Or perhaps you want to find a romantic partner. Making friends first is a great way to do that. Whatever it is your looking for defining it and write it down in detail. The greater clarity you have the clearer the steps required to achieve that goal will be. Write your goals out in detail. Describe the type of friends you're looking for. Do they like to party? Are they intelligent? Older? Describe the kind of social activities you want to be doing in your free time.

Choose a main social goal that you would like to achieve within one year. Imagine the result you dream about. Break this down into monthly, weekly, and daily milestones. For example, that could be talking to new people every day or taking a new route to work which increases your chances of meeting people. Weekly that could be going to new classes, taking up new hobbies or setting up dates, and so on. Monthly that could be checking on your progress, taking extended trips, and so on. Then yearly you're looking at the bigger vision such as finding a new best friend or your new peer group to hang out with. Use a spreadsheet to track all of this. I highly recommend Google sheets because you can access it on your phone or computer anywhere.

The keys to unlocking your goal

Metrics are going to be the keystone of this journey to keep you motivated and on track. In truth, they are the real keys to unlocking your goal. Let me tell you frankly. If you read only one part of this book, then this is going to be the most important part. Put your glasses on now! I mean it's all good and well to have a goal, but we need to act on it. Metrics will enhance the chances of you achieving your goal. They will spur the action. All roads to your social goals will come from metrics.

Now when it comes to metrics it is important to not get too detailed. Otherwise, it can overwhelm us. I want you to track one thing only. What is that one thing? The number of new people you talk to each day. Each week, track the results and see how they stack up to the other weeks' results. Try to speak to twenty to thirty people a week. If you really want to then you can add their names as well. That's a bonus for connecting with them! Now, these people do not need to be all strangers. But it does need to happen out there in the real world. Not online. Real-world experience will allow you to work on improving those important social skills such as confidence and charisma. Whilst at the same time, you will be working on reducing any of your bad social habits.

To track your metrics, create a spreadsheet with each day of the week in it. List those going downwards. Going across create sections for names, people, and notes. Each day you can record data in those columns. Try to get the names of people with whom you had conversations. If not just put an X in the name column. You can also add any important notes in the last column such as how the conversation went and if there are things which you could improve. Again, aim to talk to about twenty to thirty new people a week. Record all of your interactions with new people, even if it's just a "hi" or a "how are you". The habit of recording this data will make you more social and motivated to achieve the results.

In addition, keep taking notes about your interactions, your weak points, and the things you are working on. Those will reveal themselves during this journey so be honest and reflective with yourself. Include all your thoughts, doubts, and insecurities. Think of it like your private therapist. This will truly progress your life and social skills.

Turning the heat up

Imagine four burners on a cooking top. Each one of those represents an area of your life. We have health, relationships, money, and charity. At various points in our lives, we can turn up the heat on one of those whilst the others keep on burning but with less intensity. Having everything burning on full heat at the same time is just not possible. We burn out. To be effective we need to immerse ourselves into one or two burners at a time.

Manage your life on a macro level this way using the four burners theory. Think of it like the cycles of life. That could be for example. Going deep with health such as focusing on having great sleep, workouts, and nutrition. In the meantime, your relationship is maintained. For example, maybe that's just catching up with old friends once a week or going on a couple of dates a week.

Since our goal right now is being social it would be a good idea for you to focus on social activities as your main burner for the next month or more. Yes, you will likely have to pull back on health, money, and charity for a bit. Maybe you will get up later, work less, and so on. But realize you can come back to those and immerse yourself in them later. Right now, you're focused on making as many friends as possible. To meet the metrics each week you will need to go out a lot. Going out to the local hotspots. Going out at night. Going out to events, meetups, and clubs. All of which will be outlined in this book. Again, remember that it's for a period of immersion and you will have to leave your house to make the magic happen.

Recently I read a great book called "The Slight Edge" by Jeff Olsen. In this book, he talks about the compounding results of things we do every day. Ultimately these add up to give us a "slight edge". Inside he tells a motivational story about two sons of a wealthy businessman who is about to die. On his deathbed, he offers them two options. A penny that doubles every day for a month or one million dollars in cash right now. One son takes the million dollars cash whilst the other goes for the doubling penny. What they find out after just one month is that the one penny a day doubling each day ended up as over ten million dollars! Far more than the million dollars upfront. (Olson, 2013)

Imagine how this concept relates to your social skills. If you go out for just ten minutes a day every day, imagine how much it adds up and compounds positively to building your social skills. Quickly you will become more comfortable in social situations and become better at making a first impression. Eventually, you will be comfortable enough to stay a little longer. Eventually, you start to make new friends and integrate into new social groups. All in just ten minutes a day. Go ahead and try it. List a bunch of places to go each day. It might feel weird being alone. But it's just ten minutes. Pretend you're waiting for a friend. Go ahead, it's just ten minutes!

Realize that it will get tiring sometimes. We have to keep things fresh and stay motivated. Introverts or extroverts, we all need a good eight to nine hours of sleep a night. When we are lacking sleep, we look and feel worse. Make sure you are well rested and stick to a healthy lifestyle. Oh and a note on alcohol. Try not to get wasted. A little drink is fine but don't overdo it. Maybe at the start, you can use a little alcohol for getting in the mood. Just know your limits and when enough is enough. Then switch to water.

NEW FRIENDS

So how can we start making new friends? First, we need to start meeting them and the number one influence on this is going to be your location. I know you might have been living in the same town for years and you've gotten comfortable. But things have probably stagnated for you. Which is probably why you're reading this. If you have been struggling for a while to meet new people, then changing your location might be a good idea. Perhaps a new city or even a new country can kick start things. But what about if you're committed to a location? Maybe you're recently single with a family and a house to care for. Whatever your case is don't worry you can still hop online and start searching for things to do in your area. You can still visit the local hotspots and become more social. Indeed, it will be limited but you don't necessarily need to uproot and move house. However, you're still going to have to go out and explore some new locations. Maybe that's something as simple as going to a new supermarket or going to a new class. Incidentally, there are some well-known activities and ideas that have historically been great ways to meet new people. Let's explore them here.

Be Social

Going back to what we discussed earlier about tracking metrics I want you to keep it in mind to be much more open and social. Try to say hi to at least three people a day. This will require you to be more present at the moment so stop checking your phone or gazing at the floor and stop holding back. If it goes wrong people will forget about you within a few seconds. Realize that most people will be happy that you acknowledged them and will usually say hi back. Just be confident and if they don't reply then do not take it personally. It's just the way they are.

Being social means, you will need to be out there more and you can combine this with the things you do daily. For example, when you're going to the gym, picking up groceries, and so on. Keep it in mind to say hi to people whenever you are out and about. Many of you reading this are probably introverts and being social doesn't come naturally to you. Us introverts are going to have to force ourselves to be social. When someone is in the lift with you, start a conversation. When you see a beautiful stranger say hi to them. When you have nothing to do on a weekday evening don't get lost scrolling or watching random stuff, go out there and meet people. Personally, I have met some great friends just by saying hi or through being out there. Here are some examples of how it happened.

Steven – Steven turned out to be an amazing friend and we went out together to bars, clubs, restaurants, hikes, and good chats. I was renting an Airbnb and one day we were both using the lift at the same time. Steven seemed not too interested to chat but at that point, I had made it a habit of always talking to strangers in situations like this. I assume they are shy but still open to meeting people. For example, if someone gets into an elevator with me, they can expect some small talk. When Steven entered the lift, I engaged him in some small talk about where he was from and what he was doing there. We then exchanged numbers and hung out from there on. Small talk often leads nowhere but for the times it does it's totally worth it.

Lars – Lars was one of the most random ways of meeting people for me but he is now a great friend. Funny story. I was walking in the street, and he came up to me asking where I could buy a sim card. We were in Colombia and if you have ever been there then you will know that it is a real hassle to get a sim card there. We shared war stories of sim card experiences then parted ways. During our chat, he mentioned there was a dance class he was going to later in the evening. So, I went, and we hit it off from there.

Hotspots

By discovering the local hotspots, you can meet tons of new people. Once I stayed in a small city which appeared to be very sleepy. Turns out the local hotspot was the beach. People going there were all super friendly and so starting conversations was natural. Meeting various people there turned into invites to more activities such as volleyball, barbecues, hanging out, and much more.

Find out where people are frequenting in your area, go there and make small talk. Once you become a known face, people will enjoy having you around. This will work well in small cities or large towns where there are fewer meetups. Are there any restaurants, bars, or salons and so on that you regularly visit? Or are there any new ones you could visit? Get to know the service staff there. Chat with them and get to know their names. In addition, there will be the customers whom you regularly see there. Instead of listening to a podcast or zoning out, try to interact with them.

Sometimes you will need to go out alone. At first, it feels weird, but you get used to it and it builds your confidence. When I moved to Buenos Ares it took me a while to meet new people and for the first month, I was going out alone. During this time many events were canceled because of covid. Nevertheless, I persisted to go out and try to meet people. It was either that or staying at home and as a single person, you can't make those excuses. In Buenos Ares, I was going on many dates usually from Tinder and on the dates, I would always ask for the local hotspots where foreigners hang out. I wanted to make some foreign friends. My dates told me about some places, and I bookmarked them for each day of the week to visit. Friday night came and I went out to a hotspot alone. Whilst in the line I got chatting to a French guy. Turns out we had some mutual friends. Naturally, he introduced me to his friends inside who then invited me to another party. Max was their friend, and I shared a taxi with him. We got on well and started hanging out with each other regularly. He is now a close friend of mine.

Go out there solo if you must because people are there waiting to meet you. Ask around and mix up the places you are going to. If you keep frequenting the same places then not only will it get boring quickly you will also be limited. Find the hotspots for different nights and plan your weeks out. In addition, don't just be the night owl. There are tons of events during the day. Try some of the fairs, meetups, and numerous daytime events. Weekends will be packed with them.

Circles

I've met so many friends through my friends. My concept is that I like to have people in my social circle who always bring new people in. Before I used to seek comfort and always sit next to a familiar face. Nowadays I push myself to sit next to the new person in the group whenever they arrive. I will do my best to make a great first impression, to listen, and try to set up mutual interests that give us good reasons to keep in contact. Eventually from this habit, your contacts list fills up and you will always have someone to go out with. Keep on expanding your social circle. Don't censor or judge anyone out too early on. Remember they can always lead you to new friends.

Dating

This is a funny one. I know usually you're going on a date with romantic intentions. But it doesn't always work out that way. Sometimes you go on a date and that sexual chemistry isn't there. But in these cases, you might still have a friendship to establish. If you're not interested in pursuing something romantic but you still enjoy their company, then let them know you value their friendship. Work on building that friendship. If you're clear that you will just be friends, then it takes out the confusion and allows a great friendship to blossom. Later, you can start to invite each other to events or to meet each other's friends. Naturally, both of your social circles will grow. Also, you can ask them for tips on the local scene of where to go. Just like I talked about earlier.

Online

Nowadays we spend so much time online. Most of it is probably wasted but it can also be a great way to connect with people. Interesting people whom you can meet up with in real life. Make sure you have a great online profile. Keep it updated and fresh with pictures. Start by joining various groups and forums of interest. Post and engage with the people there. Groups are an excellent way to meet new people. For example, there are tons of walking groups out there. My parents who are in their sixties have met many people in their age group through walking groups. Usually, it's the older crowd going on these and it makes a great activity to get into long conversations and make deep connections.

Big cities will have an abundance of groups and meetups. But smaller ones do too. Especially for activities such as walking groups. Just hop onto Google and search for events and groups in your area. Additionally, search on Facebook and www.meetup.com. I also want to give a bonus tip for Facebook. It can be an incredibly distracting tool. You go there looking for events and end up looking at someone you dated in old photos. To keep yourself productive, use it on Google chrome with the news feed blocker extension enabled. Then you can stick to only checking out events. In the events section, you will also be notified of your friends' birthdays. Send them birthday wishes to keep yourself fresh in their minds should any upcoming events occur that they might invite you to.

Furthermore, you can find hotspots on Instagram and follow their pages for any updates on events. There will always be ones specific to your city so sign up for those. People will post things that could be event opportunities or chances to hang out with new people. Build up a connection with people there. Keep up to date with what is going on. Often you will find people arranging meetups that you could go to. Be open-minded and go for it. Keep your interests as broad as possible. Each week or every other day I keep a lookout for upcoming events listed on Facebook, Google, and Meetup. These are the best sources of new events. Look for the popular ones and tick to receive notifications about them.

Search for events online. Whenever I go to a new city I always search for events. Networking events are a great start. I met one of my best friends at one. Interesting because he is the kind of guy I would usually avoid. Loud and eccentric. I remember seeing him at many of the networking events. Turns out he is one of the most well-connected people I have ever met!

Anyway, eventually, we got chatting and he invited me to his housewarming party. Through him, I met so many more people and we just kept bumping into each other at events or out and about. The more out there you are, the more chances of meeting people you have. Plus it goes to show that you should not be too judgmental of people early on. It takes time to truly get to know someone. I discovered that behind the loud and eccentric character he is a thoughtful and inspiring person.

Keep saying yes to more social events and exploring. Saying yes more is a key to more social engagements and meeting people. I know it can be easy to get set in your ways. Yeah, it's nice to lay in bed and watch some podcasts for the evening. But that's not life. Saying yes leads you to more life. Just try it for a few weeks. When people invite you out, always say yes. It can open so many new doors for you. Don't judge things too harshly. Have an open mind. Be an easy person to be around. Smile a lot. Agree a lot. Say yes, a lot. The number of times I have been on the fence about going out then I change my mind and magic happens.

Volunteer

Volunteering is a really great way to meet some kindhearted spirits. In fact, many successful people frequently volunteer. There are many volunteering options available. Just hop onto Google and do a search. Furthermore, keep performing random acts of kindness and make a conscious effort to be more kind. Hold doors open, say please, and thank you. Remember that charity begins at home.

Sports

Sports are an excellent way to stay healthy and meet people at the same time. There are hundreds of sports to choose from. Have an open mind to this and seek out those that tend to have more people. In addition, find the peak times. For me, I train in martial arts. Usually, I attend an evening class because there are more people to connect with. However, you might also find people on your level at other times. That's cool too because they will have similar schedules to you.

The gym is also a great way to meet people. Most people have their heads down and are anti-social. Try too not to be like that. In between sets just relax and look around. Stay off your phone. Acknowledge and say hi to other people when you enter the gym. Ask people how they are. Get to know the staff. Go to some of the classes. That's how I have met many friends.

Dance is great too. There are so many styles of dance that you can try out. From Tango to Salsa these are all great ways to meet a wide range of new people. At the events, you will be encouraged to interact with all the people there. Over time as you keep going each week, you're going to forge new relationships. Now don't be too picky. Because even though someone might not be your cup of tea, they can however lead you to new people and their circle. Search your area for dance classes and give them a try.

Search on Facebook and Google for sports or classes in your area. Here are a few ideas: tennis, golf, martial arts, board games, archery, sailing, and dance. The list goes on and on. Don't worry if you have no skills. Just be honest about it. Tell the people you're here to learn. Or even better take a course. Go out there and try.

Language exchanges

Almost every major city is going to feature a bunch of different language exchanges. These can range from intimate tables of language exchanges to a more party-style event. Check out whatever is in your area. Try them all out and keep on going. Each week you will meet people from a wide range of backgrounds. There will be travelers and locals alike who you can connect with. It's great because they can show you around their city or you can explore new places together.

Toastmasters

Toastmasters is a group of people who meet up either monthly or weekly to practice their public speaking skills. It is an international organization with groups running across the world. Every major city will have one or more groups. Usually, they are monthly. Personally, I prefer the weekly options because it exposes me to more opportunities and people. If you're in a big city you can join multiple. The Toastmaster membership allows this.

Each week about three members will have the opportunity to present a five-to-eight-minute speech. For more advanced speakers it can be for an extended time of up to twenty minutes. In addition, there are some on-the-spot activities and games for the other participants attending. I highly recommend Toastmasters as an activity to add to your social calendar. Public speaking is directly correlated with confidence, charisma, and social skills. Furthermore, you meet people who attend the groups each time and make new friends.

Travel

One of the best ways to meet a ton of new people is to go traveling. If you're single and have the chance, then go for it. This will truly take you out of your comfort zone to go out there and make new friends. Explore the world. My life as a digital nomad allows me to get up and move to new places. You might think this limits the depth of my relationships, but I feel it adds to them. My strategy isn't just a few weeks here and there. Instead, I set up a base in a new city for a minimum of three months. One month isn't enough, that's usually when the ball just begins rolling. When you arrive in a new place the first month is spent sightseeing and getting a feel for it. During that time you will probably have some hit, miss, and false start friendships. The second month is usually when you start to meet people who you're going to connect much better with. As time progresses those relationships deepen.

Time and distance create a sense of appreciation. I always come back to a place I used to live with a fresh mind and newfound appreciation. Essentially it keeps things fresh. I know this lifestyle isn't for everyone but if you're single and work remotely I encourage you to give it a shot. I also want to mention that if you're otherwise committed then you too will find what's inside this book to be useful. One doesn't necessarily need to move to the other side of the world to make things happen. Maybe just moving to a new area of your city can freshen things up a bit. Ultimately a move gives you a new lease on life, new surroundings, new opportunities, and new friends.

One of the ways you could do that is to negotiate to work remotely with your current boss. Tell them you will work better from home and that you would love to prove it to them. As long as you hit their targets, I'm sure they will be happy for you to do this. I know one guy who negotiated to spend six months of each year in

Brazil. When the snow starts to fall in Europe he heads for the sunny beaches of Rio de Janeiro. Alternatively, start investing in a side hustle that generates income regardless of where you ate. Now, this topic is beyond the scope of this book. But in brief, here are some proven ways of making money online.

- Drop shipping – buy products on one website and sell them for more on another website. Requires no inventory and can be done from anywhere. Will require a decent size of investment and requires some risk.

- Publishing – invest in book writing and sell books from anywhere in the world. Books are digital assets, so no inventory is required. Even printing it is done on demand by a third party. Requires solid understanding and business savvy.

- Crypto – buy cryptocurrency at a good price and hold it until it appreciates.

Ideally, it keeps growing in value although it can be a volatile market.

- Trading – buy stocks at low prices and trade them for profit. Requires studying the market trends and analysis. Realize that to succeed you will need to understand the stocks you are trading.

- Merch – many websites offer print-on-demand where you can list an item. A customer buys it and the order is sent to a warehouse that manufactures and distributes it for you. Competitive but requires no inventory so it's both passive and location independent.

Ultimately this business or remote work will give you more freedom and flexibility to have your own time to pursue a satisfying social life wherever you are in the world.

FIRST IMPRESSIONS

As a natural response to meeting someone for the first time we make quick judgments which are often inaccurate. Especially online where we are seeing just a snapshot of someone's life. According to a 2006 study published in Psychological Science, in under a tenth of a second of seeing someone for the very first time we make quick conclusions about a person's qualities. (Willis & Todorov, 2006) This includes attributes such as friendliness, trustworthiness, honesty and much more. Known as The Serial Positioning Effect it explains how we tend to remember more so the things at the beginning and at the end. Whether we like it or not this tendency is built within us from way back in evolutionary times as a way of assessing whether a stranger would become an ally or an enemy. (How to Make a Good First Impression: Expert Tips and Tricks, 2022)

Although they can be misleading, first impressions often end up influencing how we form our judgment of a person. Once we have formed one it is like a filter which everything a person does goes through, and it can take a long time to change. In fact, all your relationships are heavily influenced by the quality of the first impression you make. When you can make a friendly first impression people will feel more comfortable being around you. Naturally they will be more than happy to introduce you to their friends. But sometimes your first impression of a person might be of them being untrustworthy. As such everything they do from then on will be viewed through a filter of untrust. Fortunately, there are some proven ways to make a better first impression. To begin I will explain two important characteristics which have a massive influence on first impressions. Following on I will present you with some of the finer details of making a great first impression. (Shortsleeve, 2018)

Confidence

According to the Merriam-Webster dictionary "Confidence is a feeling or consciousness of one's powers or of reliance on one's circumstances." (Merriam-Webster, 2022)

Confidence is the belief someone has in themselves that they can overcome any challenges they may face. Imagine someone who can be themselves all the time. Seemingly intense social situations don't appear to bother them in the slightest. They can rock up to any event alone and easily talk with new people or even travel to a new country alone. A confident person has a strong self of self is sure of their capabilities and speaks their truth. Those who can project confidence are great at making strong first impressions, dealing with pressure, and overcoming both personal and professional challenges. Furthermore, it is an attractive personality trait that helps to make others more comfortable being around them. Of course, this is very appealing to be around. We all love to be around people who own their identities. It's charming.

Realize that confidence isn't something we are born with at a fixed level. In fact, it can be improved over time. So how does one become more confident? Body language is a good place to start. Stand upright. No more slouching. Smile more and use wide, slower movements. Speak more loudly and utilize tonality. In addition, confidence is grown through experience. Instead of avoiding difficult emotions, acknowledge and explore them. The more we can challenge ourselves and overcome those fears the stronger we can grow. Take a trip on your own now and then. Go out alone. I want to emphasize this again. Try going to a big event or to a club alone. Just the thought of this is going to give people massive anxiety. If they make it out alone, upon arrival they will usually want to escape the minute they enter. It feels like everyone is looking at you and they know you're alone. Realize this, no one cares! They might think about it for a second then they go back to worrying about how they look or thinking about talking to someone. Look, try this. Make up some story that your friends went to another place and you really wanted to come here. As soon as you enter, smile. Keep smiling and slowly move around the place. Start talking to anyone and everyone. This will get you out of your head. Ask obvious questions so that you know the answer. For example, where is the toilet or what time is it? Order a drink and talk to the bar staff. Remember it's all social interaction that puts you in a social mood. Talk to more strangers at any time in any place. Start to speak up for yourself and get comfortable speaking your truth regardless of what the outcome might be. Find out the things which bring you social anxiety and challenge yourself to try them. I know it won't be easy at first but afterward, you will feel much more confident in yourself. Keep at it

Continue to set and meet goals both in your personal and professional life. The process of goal setting and progression will naturally instill you with more confidence as you make progress. When you're succeeding in life and work it makes you more confident which spills over as a positive effect on your social life. It goes without saying but always work on living your best life. That's the way of a confident person.

Remember that once you become a confident person it's important to not overdo it. Overconfidence can come off as arrogant, cocky, and narcissistic. All of which are social life killers because no one likes to hang out with someone who has an inflated ego. There just isn't any space for it! You don't need to show off or brag. Imagine a person with a cool and calm demeanor whatever the situation. They believe in themselves and don't need to prove it to anyone. That is true confidence. (Psychology Today, 2022)

Charisma

According to the Merriam-Webster dictionary, charisma is "a special magnetic charm or appeal." (Merriam-Webster, 2022)

Think of charisma as a trait that attracts and influences others. However, realize that it is not some mystery or magic which you either have or don't have. On the contrary, it can be learned and cultivated through time and practice. Imagine the person who is fully themselves. Charisma isn't necessarily about someone being loud and charming. It is more the art of expressing yourself in an authentic and calibrated manner. If you're a nerd for example you can still be one just without the social anxieties and bad habits. Just look at Elon Musk. He is a nerd, but he is also very charismatic. That's mostly because he owns who is and doesn't hold back on it. He embraces it and makes it cool.

Charismatic people are fun to be around. They leave you wanting to hang out with them again and again. When thinking of a charismatic person, rock stars, leaders and actors often come to mind. But it's not just for the rich, famous, and successful. We all too can become charismatic. Being able to influence and attract others is a highly useful social skill. This power is embodied in the way a charismatic person speaks and acts. They project confidence and portray expressive body language. They are optimistic, enthusiastic, and passionate in addition to being assertive. Essentially, they know who they are and they aren't afraid to show it. As such they stand out from the crowd and in their own unique way.

Charisma is not a set thing you're born with although extroverts tend to be more charismatic. Some people have tons of charisma and some are less than others. The point is that it can all be learned. So how do you become more charismatic? Make use of the specific techniques and characteristics of charisma. For example, speak with more emotion. Use metaphors to describe things, and situations, and express and share emotions. Practice nonverbal's such as gestures, facial expressions, and body language to express yourself. Socialize more and push yourself to act without restrictions on your behavior. Now that's not about being rude or obnoxious rather it is about having fewer filters on what you should say and do. It's like wearing a bright pink shirt to an all-white party! Realize that charisma is like a muscle that needs to be worked out. The more out there you are the more you can work on it. (Psychology Today, 2022)

Social freedom

Social freedom is an effective tool for building more confidence and charisma, but it is often misunderstood. Most people assume it's about acting like a fool in public. Really there is so much misleading nonsense on the internet about it. True social freedom is more like a combination of charisma and confidence. Wherein the person with social freedom is confident in being themselves one hundred percent whatever the situation. It's the person being able to state their honest opinion. Or being able to talk calmly in front of a large crowd. They have a positive mindset and believe in themselves.

So how do you achieve such a state? Well, you could do cartwheels in the street, or you could work on identifying what your weak points are. Go ahead and ask yourself do you hold back in certain social situations? Why is that? Are you for example worried about being judged? Or maybe you feel shy around new people. Work on finding out what that reason is. Remember to always be journaling on your journey. Use it as a growth tool to brainstorm and write about becoming a better you.

Once you have identified your weak points

which will come about through regular journaling you can then work on improving them. Ask yourself. What is the opposite of that weak point? What would a person who is the opposite of this look like? How can you get from where you are now to that point? I can tell you. Probably it is going to involve exposure. In fact the more exposure the better. If for example talking to groups is a big thing for you then go to more group events. Take up a dance class where you will be put on the spot. All eyes will be on you, and you will have to introduce yourself to the group. Add in some weekly toastmasters where you're going to be talking to large groups each week.

Keep on exposing yourself to group activities and learn to get comfortable with them. It's not about acting a fool in front of people to desensitize yourself. Behavior like that will yes make you de-sensitized but you will also end up looking like a weirdo. Better to work on bringing out your core personality. Be the person who people want to have around. Not the weirdo they want to avoid. Speak your mind but don't be rude. There are various ways you can say things more politely without being blunt. You can have social etiquette and manners whilst being honest. What I am saying is to work on saying exactly what you want. Speak your truth. Let go of attachment to wanting to please people or to fit in. Again, yes you will turn people off and alienate some others. But ultimately it will bring you closer in alignment with the people you should be with and the life you should be living. Now for the finer details of making a great first impression.

Appearance

First things first. When it comes to the finer details of making a great first impression your appearance matters. I'm sure you've heard those often-quoted statements that body language accounts for the majority of all communication. Indeed, that's true and so what's on the body? Clothes! Therefore, we must make a conscious effort to dress well. It's not necessarily about wearing a suit or a formal dress. We can still look respectable in casual clothes. Remember that it all depends on the context. Are you going on a date? Are you going to an interview? Or are you going out with a new group of friends? Clearly, for an interview, you wouldn't dress the same as you would for going out with friends. Understand the context first and then dress for the occasion.

The most important thing regarding clothes is to make sure they fit well. Nothing should be too baggy or too tight. For example, men's t-shirts should be tight around the biceps and hang a decent amount below the waist. Too many men wear t-shirts that are loose on the arms and that rest up too high. In worst cases, they expose a belly! Now if you have a cool belt maybe it looks ok. Or if the t-shirt and jeans are the same color it looks fine. Jeans and trousers work well being more well fit and tighter. Buy some flexible jeans which are more elastic. They are also super comfy and will mold well to your legs. For guys, this gives a more defined v shape which is attractive. You can get away with a loser t-shirt or shirt then. Or you can wear some nice simple black or chino cotton trousers. Add in formal shirts and shorts for a trip to the beach or out at the park. This looks classy and is comfortable.

For women dresses look best that accentuate the waist-to-hip ratio. Nice and tight round the waist. Don't worry if you're a little on the chubby side you can make use of designs with bigger belts and fits. Shop around and find the shops that fit your body type. Some sizes in certain shops will work well for you and others won't. Strike a balance of comfort and style. You want to feel and look good. So, try things on and avoid any maybes. That means it's a good fit, looks good, and feels good. Feeling good is important because for example you might live in a hot country and find a shirt that looks good but is made from heavy material. The moment you step outside it's going to boil you up! Find your ideal. Remember to tick the three boxes. No maybes!

- Looks great
- Feels great
- Fits great

Colors are important too. Some skin tones work well with others, and some don't. Personally, I am very light-skinned so darker colors work well on me. For darker skin tones you can get away with brighter colors. I would also recommend going for plainer clothes with great fits rather than extravagant designs. Those items are rarer, and you might end up bumping into someone wearing the same outfit. God forbid lol. Plus, they will bring you a lot of attention. But if that's what you want then go for it. Usually what works well is plain designs with some small details. Try not to go for more than say three colors in a design. For example, I like to wear jeans with cool little patterns on them in the same color. Or with some small tears in them. Or maybe a shirt with a double button. These small and classy little details work well. Again, it's up to you.

Finally, at the bottom end, shoes are super important. You can have a great outfit that might be trashed by some scruffy shoes. In fact, an average outfit can look amazing with great shoes. Add in a nice watch or jewelry to compliment everything like the icing on a cake. A casual outfit with a classy watch makes you look super stylish. Or maybe you have a cool little chain to go over your plain t-shirt. Find what looks great on you for the occasion. Dress well and feel confident.

Etiquette

Etiquette is underrated and something we all need to have. It's not about trying to be royal or prestigious. Rather it's about being a decent and polite human. Be the kind of person you want to invite over and introduce to your friends. Now there are certain habits that are truly sins of interactions. In fact, they are downright rude and will scare people away from you like a rabid dog. Neither friend nor foe nor stranger should be in the presence of these. Keep them to yourself in private!

Swearing is a common one and it is a form of language laziness. People all too often use swearing as a filler. Work on getting rid of it and use pauses instead. Never ever fart, burp, spit or pick your nose in front of others. When eating never talk with your mouth full. Keep your breath fresh. Bad breath is very off-putting for other people. I'm sure you probably had that experience of talking to someone with bad breath before. You probably want to avoid them. Bad breath usually comes from food getting stuck in between our teeth and then fermenting. Nasty stuff! Make sure you floss at least twice a day and after meals. Furthermore, if you're out and about all day your breath can get stale. Keep a set of mints or chewing gum in your pocket to freshen up your breath. Or at least brush your teeth twice a day, and don't forget to floss!

Finally, make sure you smell great. Don't be lazy, if you have just finished a workout at the gym then go take a shower before heading out to lunch. Also, take a shower before the gym so that you look fresh to the people there. If someone has a bad odor it's off-putting. If your shirts smell all musty, wash them again. Wear a nice cologne. It doesn't have to be some super expensive brand name stuff. There are some great colognes available at department stores for decent prices. Go test them. Better still take someone attractive with you and ask for their opinion. Splash a little on every time you go out. In addition, always use underarm deodorant or roll on. Stay fresh because it all boosts your confidence.

Attitude

A great attitude creates a great first impression. When you have a positive attitude people will be more likely to perceive you in a positive way. On the flip side, if you are having a bad day, you're going to give off bad vibes. Attitude is reflected in your face, body language, and overall vibe. Many of us all too often have a serious look on our faces. Even though we might feel good on the inside, the look on your face can come off as unfriendly. Shift that and keep a smile on your face. This makes you more approachable and therefore perceived as being friendlier.

Work on your attitude. Try to be more positive and uplifting. You can work on this by first analyzing your influences. Are you watching a lot of negative news? Or are you consuming uplifting content? Are you mixing with positive people? Or are they bringing you down? Cultivate more positivity into your life and it will manifest in your attitude. Daily I work on this by doing an exercise called positive journaling. The process involves journaling about any positive experiences I have had during the last twenty-four hours. No ifs, buts, or negatives are allowed. What you will find from regularly doing this exercise is that it enhances your mindset to focus on the positive which ultimately affects your attitude. In the end, we all like to be around positive-minded people.

Read the room

When you enter a new social environment take the time to gather yourself. If you have time beforehand do your research on any upcoming events you might be attending. This will help you to understand the environment and the context. Additionally, it will make you more confident when you attend since you will be well prepared for the occasion. When you arrive, read the room or environment in which you happen to be. Observe how the people are interacting there. Are they talking loudly and being extroverted? Or is it a more intimate style of communication? Get a good read on the situation and then start to act appropriately. Make sure your conversation style and mannerisms match that context. For example, many of us can get carried away with business chats on social occasions. Or being too informal in work contexts. Generally, you should maintain a polite and professional manner for workplace contexts and so on.

Saving bad first impressions

Now if you've made the mistake of making a bad first impression then don't worry because it is something you can recover from. Yes, it will take some time and effort, but it is possible to recover from a bad first impression. First, accept your mistake and identify the cause of it. Admitting our mistakes can be hard. But when you are humble enough to do that, you can make progress. If it is necessary, apologize for your mistake. Maybe you were rude or uncalibrated. Own your mistake and apologize for it. This will prove to others that you're self-aware and humble enough to be a good friend to them. Don't dwell on that first bad impression. Once you have accepted it and owned it, start to focus on the actions you will take to improve upon it. Maybe that's being a better listener or being more optimistic.

Additionally, we should try to always end on a high note. Make people laugh, smile, or inspire them with a positive story. Try to always end conversations in those ways. Remember we make impressions from the start and end points so always make people remember you in a positive way. With practice, you will become a master of making a great first impression that lasts.

STARTING CONVERSATIONS

Every day as you step out into the world there are hundreds of potential conversations available to you. Some people seem to be natural at starting a conversation. Whilst for the rest of us it can be a real struggle. However, it is a skill that can be learned which will help you in a wide range of social situations. From meeting new clients to making new friends or even for potential romantic interests. Becoming better at starting conversations is the gateway to friendships. Following here are some excellent ways to start conversations.

Attention

Most people are stuck in their heads not making eye contact or acknowledging anyone. Realize that starting a conversation is on you. I know it can feel high pressure to hear this but the more you practice the easier it gets. Imagine that every person you come across could be your next new friend. But first, you will need to get their attention. Look out for people who seem open to talking. Watch them until they make eye contact. But don't stare too long, they are either open or not. Also, you can smile, wave, or say hey to get their attention. Then leave a pause giving enough time to grab their attention.

Once they make eye contact with you smile and say, "hi" or "how's it going". Some people might just look down or ignore you. Remember to not take it personally. They probably aren't interested in talking to anyone right now. Experience and intuition will help you to read people and determine who is open to having conversations. Pay attention to the intuition you feel about people. Maybe they have a bad vibe, or maybe you are drawn to them. Trust and develop your instincts. Daily meditation will help you to sharpen your intuition and in turn, make you more self-aware.

The Art of Small talk

When you open up to people and if they respond well, you can start out with some small talk. To begin keep things light and non-personal. The best kind of small talk is situational. Usually for example we default to small talk about the weather. Isn't it hot today? Or the rain is awful this week and so on. This is excellent for new conversations with strangers. For example, you might be watching sports at the pub. Then it is easy to get talking about the game. Or you might be having lunch and it's easy to engage in small talk about the food. Or maybe you're at the gym and you ask to use a machine or to do a set. Look for the obvious ways to start situational conversations. Throw the bait out there and hopefully, they bite. If not, no worries again don't take it personally.

Introductions

Maybe you caught the eyes of someone at an event. Or there is a new person where you work. Introducing yourself can be a smooth way of starting a conversation. Obviously, there should be a good reason for you to connect with them and the context will determine the situation. For example, people tend to introduce themselves at work events or at social gatherings with mutual friends. Furthermore, try to introduce yourself to any new people you come across. Challenge yourself. I know it can feel weird but think about it most people love it when someone has the courage to introduce themselves. Just go up and say, "hi, I saw you're here often my name is" …. Don't have any expectations. Just a smile on your face combined with a confident greeting.

Information

Another easy way to start a conversation is to ask a person whom you want to talk to for information. Even though you might already know the answer, it is still a great conversation starter. For example, you could ask for information about an event, directions, or the surroundings that you happen to be in. This can easily lead to the deeper conversation since it has content for you to dive into. In addition, if you notice someone needs help, then be a kind human and offer them your help. Maybe for example you're good with languages and you see someone lost in translation. Or maybe they look lost, and you offer them direction.

When we ask others for their opinion it shows them that we respect and value their thoughts. When people are knowledgeable about a subject, they will be more than happy to respond and share their expertise. Remember to always ask open-ended questions which are relevant to the scenario and settings. Keep going deeper. Stay engaged. Let them know you understand them by rephrasing what they say to you along with eye contact and questions. People are there to help you. Just speak up and ask them. Ask that stranger for advice, to borrow a pen, or to direct you. Remember to get out of your head and into the world.

Running out of things to say

Running out of things to say can dry up your conversations. Here is a hack to jump-start your mind the next time it goes blank. Think of the metaphor HPM (history, philosophy, and metaphor). This will help you to never run out of things to say. Use it to respond to statements, situations, environments and so. Respond with something related to your history (a personal story), philosophy (your opinion on something), or a metaphor (what it makes you think of). Never run out of things to say again! You can thank me later.

In addition, have your stories prepared in advance. What have you been up to? Where have you been? How was your weekend? And so on. Instead of saying things like "not much" or "it was ok". Prepare a few stories in advance. Maybe you didn't do much except watch a movie. Talk about that movie. At least it gives the conversation a little fuel. You could say yeah, I watched this cool new movie. Boom there is a thread of conversation started. Or maybe you chilled all weekend. You could say I had a quiet one. I was pretty burned out from all the work. Talk about what you did to recover. Planning in advance will ensure that your conversations stay alive and don't die before they have a chance to get going.

Things to avoid

Finally, I want to highlight some negative aspects and elements of communication that you must be aware of. Become conscious of them and if they apply to your work on eradicating them. The end goal is to become a smoother, more charming, and charismatic person. In turn, this will make you more likable and more people will want to become your friend.

Conversations should be smooth and not jarred by the interruption. Give people the chance to speak. Allow them plenty of time. Don't rush into saying what you want. Be flexible. When your moment comes then say what you need to. I know some people talk too much and you can work around that by using body language such as smiling or gesturing to make your point of when to come in. But never interrupt them midway through what they are saying. Think of it like a sixty-forty ratio of them speaking and you listening. Sometimes you will have to gauge their pace and how they articulate points. But don't worry you will get better at this intuitive skill through regular social practice.

Don't be rude or overbearing. Usually, the common cause of this is a lack of empathy. Be polite, open, and confident. We warm to people who come off as warm and friendly. When we talk too much and don't listen enough, this communicates to the other person that we aren't that interested in what they have to say. Learn to listen more and learn when to make your point or to reply. Sometimes people will just want you to listen. At the same time, you should not try too hard, it might seem obvious and come off as insincere. Be authentic and natural.

Focus on positive conversations that are progressive and valuable. If you tend to gossip about others, then just realize you will probably also be gossiped about. Live by the sword and die by the sword. The same is true with gossip, those who gossip are gossiped about. There is a well-known quote that goes something like this; 'small minds talk about people; big minds talk about ideas.' Live by those words. When you talk about others, focus on the positives or at least be constructive in your criticism. Be willing to say whatever you would to someone's face that you do when they are not there with you. If you have nothing good to say, then say nothing. Also, you need to be aware that there are certain topics that can be polarizing and lead to bad interactions. People will likely have strong opinions about such topics so with new friends it's a good idea to avoid discussing them.

Religion, race, gossip, politics, sex, gender, salary, and age. Those kinds of subjects can be quite controversial and often lead to disagreement.

Try to keep your phone away when you are present with other people. Work on the art of conversation. In modern times the biggest distraction is our phones. I know we have all seen countless people at dinner on their phones. Work on going deeper with the people you're around. Work on being more present at the moment. We could all do with a little digital detox now and then. Especially when we are with others. Those Instagram notifications can wait. There should be minimal distractions. The point is to stay engaged and not float out into the background. Staying engaged will keep you alert and present to the moment of being social. Now you don't need to get high or drink to do that. Sure, a drink or two is fine but don't get wasted. Anymore will only degrade your conversations and your health.

BODY LANGUAGE

Body language has been quoted and proven many times to be where most of the communication between people takes place. Like a slap in the face from Will Smith, it can really help you to stand out. In this chapter, I will outline some of the key elements of body language, plus some things to avoid.

Positive body language

There is positive body language and there is negative body language. The difference is how they make you feel and how you are perceived. Negative body language such as frowning, arms folded, or being closed off will push people away and make you feel in a negative state. Positive body language that is open and welcoming makes you feel much better and is more inviting. Naturally, this will help you to make a great first impression and in turn have great interactions. Stand or sit up straight with your head held up. Keep a smile on your face. Make great eye contact. Avoid any negative body language such as the crossing of the arms or legs.

Touch

Touch can help us to build rapport and to hold a person's attention. It's like we have hit a new level of a connection with someone once they have touched us. Obviously, you should never touch people inappropriately, especially anyone whom you don't know well. With strangers, you can use light touches on the arms and shoulder areas. These are the safe zones. Tap them gently here if you feel they are zoning out. Think of it as snapping them back into awareness. But don't hit them! Just use light tapping. For closer friends, you can let those touches last a little longer. Maybe a hand placed on the shoulder or an arm around them is a great way of showing affection to your close friends.

Handshakes, fist bumps, hugs, and kisses we can use as introductions or meetings with old friends. Always make use of these because they are great for forming bonds even with old friends. When you shake hands offer a firm but not crushing handshake. Oh, and here is a tip for handshakes. Warm your hands first. Go ahead and rub them together. People with a warm and firm but not too firm handshake will receive a better impression than a cold, stiff, or wet handshake.

Hand gestures

We can use hand gestures to underline and accentuate our words. We can point things out. We can convey size, depth, and more. Love or hate him, Donald Trump has some very effective hand gestures. His style is very dominant which he uses to underline his points. However, if you hate him so much then observe how Eddie

Murphy keeps his audiences locked in during his early comedy shows. Low-key body language is the key there. Comedians are masters of body language. Study them.

When it comes to hand gestures, don't overdo it. Be calm, succinct, and concise. No erratic movements. Synchronicity works well. Keep your hands loosely at the sides or held together in front just above your waist allowing you to gesture easily and naturally from there.

Eye contact

Eye contact is a way of showing respect whilst conveying honesty and engagement with another person whom you are communicating with. It shows them that you're paying attention to what they say which will make them like you more. During your conversations maintain regular eye contact. Attention spans are dependent on it. Watch interviews with Mark Zuckerberg. He keeps it locked in because he studies it. Incidentally, he is currently developing a video calling software that will utilize eye contact features. Something that current applications such as Zoom, or Skype are missing.

Maintain eye contact. Now don't constantly stare. Naturally, you should break it now and then for example when you think or speak. This will push and pull attention to keep things more engaging. But don't disengage for too long. Especially if you're listening. Pay attention! Leil Lowndes the bestselling author of "How To Talk To Anyone" suggests a 60/40 mix, with 60% eye contact being the ideal amount. (Lowndes, 2003) In addition, nod to stay tuned in. You can nod subtly when people are talking which will show them that you're genuinely interested in what they have to say. We are all drawn to people who show interest so convey your interest to them.

Smile

Smiling with sincerity makes people feel welcome and at ease. A sincere smile reaches right up to the eyes. A fake smile is simply the lips curving. Practice smiling with sincerity. Your eyes should crinkle a little. You don't need a huge toothy smile. Just a slight up curve and a crinkle in the eyes. Make this your default expression. Check in the mirror and on camera until you have it nailed. You want to have a cool, calm, and approachable demeanor. You should also feel the emotions of positivity when you smile. This will make your smiles much more sincere and warm.

Smile at new people when you meet them. Smile at strangers when you pass them. Keep a slight smile on your face when you listen. It will soften up your expression making you appear less cold and more approachable. When I was a DJ, I learned this trick. Always keep smiling. When I didn't, people would tell me my music wasn't that good. But when I was smiling all night people would praise my music. Furthermore, it all compounded in a positive cycle of making me and other people around me feel better.

Try filming yourself talking to the camera.

Recording yourself on camera each week is an excellent way to improve your appearance and body language. Let me share something personal with you. I started doing this about seven years ago. In the beginning, I noticed that my face was way too serious. I also noticed that one of my lower teeth was crooked which almost made it look like I was toothless on the bottom row. Recording myself convinced me to have my teeth fixed and they look way better now. Recording myself also helped me to work on my eye contact which was all over the place before. Then there was my voice which was way too mono and boring. I encourage you to do the same. In fact, you could even take it a step further and upload them to YouTube for feedback. Stick with it and in a year or more you will see massive improvements.

Mirroring

Mirroring is a technique that can help to establish rapport with another person. Essentially it involves copying others' body language, gestures, and movements. This closely aligns us with them and gives us the feeling of having a rapport with them. When in new situations with strangers it is an effective tactic. For example, at job interviews or at networking events. Maybe they cross a leg over and then you do the same.

Now it's important to say here that you shouldn't be too obvious when mirroring. People might clock onto it and think your behavior is weird. So, for example, don't instantly copy them in an identical way. Rather slowly shift into a more subtle mirroring of them. Follow their pace and keep trying to align with their body language, gestures, and movements. You will find it does wonders for your interactions. Practice mirroring with some YouTube videos and get comfortable with the subtle art of mirroring.

Space

Space can create comfort or discomfort. When we stand too close to a new person it can create discomfort. I know one guy who always gets way too close. Literally, I must take a step back from him. But then he goes forward! Even though he was a nice enough guy I disliked him because it came off as weird. A good distance for one-to-one conversations is arm's reach away. Anything closer would be a little seductive or otherwise weird. Also, too much space can also be a bad thing. When someone is too far away not only is it leaving a disconnected feeling, but it also might be hard to hear them. Furthermore, avoid standing face to face. That can be too confrontational. Generally, a ninety-degree angle is what friends speak at with heads turning to the side slightly to talk. This is good for standing. For sitting you can establish rapport face to face since you will probably be having dinner or drinks seated at a table.

Speech tips

Tonality, Amplitude, and Speed

Utilizing tonality, amplitude and speed is an amazing way to lock people's attention onto you when you are talking. When it comes to tonality we can go up in pitch or we can go down in pitch. Too many of us speak in a monotone which makes it boring for the listener. Meanwhile, our points are not clearly defined enough. Make use of pitch to emphasize your points such as at the end of a sentence. When you conclude a point come down in pitch a little bit. Or when you want to exaggerate something, shift the pitch up a bit.

Amplitude can be used to grab attention. Mix it up between loud and quiet. For example, during a suspenseful part of a story speak quietly to lock people's attention. Then ramp up the volume into a finale. Obviously, we don't want to be too dramatic unless it fits your personality. Subtleness is the key here. In addition, make sure you are speaking loudly enough. Many people struggle to be heard. You might think others are ignoring you, but the truth is you're not speaking loudly enough. Stop caring if people overhear you. Again, this is a path towards social freedom. If you think talking quietly is an issue for you (which it probably is) then focus on it and grade yourself on it each day. Try to talk twenty to fifty percent louder.

Speed added in with the other elements is a final addition to capturing and holding your listeners' attention. We can speak slowly or quickly. Mixing the two together is a great combination. Use them in combination to articulate points of interest. To gloss over highlights of a story or to draw out the suspense. Again, be subtle and not over the top. For extreme examples listen to how sports show hosts announce winners. Practice your three tools of tonality, amplitude, and speed.

Pauses

Pauses allow us to be understood, to engage, and add suspense. Be sure to add them to your interactions. Whenever you steamroll someone and just rattle on then they will probably get lost in another trail of thought. Now if you're a person with social anxiety, then you will probably rush to get your words out. Realize that without enough pauses you will not be properly understood, and your words will have little meaning.

Pauses are also great for creating suspense. Practice adding some after you have made a point. Get comfortable with having that space to hang there. Some people be will slowly understand what you said so give them time to digest the information. Once you have made your point or said what you wanted then to leave that pause. It can give you time to think and time for the subject matter to fall. Don't try to fill those silences in with any additional useless information. Utilize the power of the pause to create tension and to let you're your points settle in.

CONNECTING

When we open to new people there is an opportunity to connect with them and potentially make new friends. For this to happen our connection needs to be worthwhile. These days engaging in conversation is rare. Human interaction has become less common as we are more engaged with our devices. Brains have become overstimulated and focused on screens instead of other people. But having deep, meaningful, and engaging conversations is much more satisfying and beneficial.

Become curious about all the people you interact with. This will keep both you and them engaged with each other. Listening to someone talk with passion can be energizing Whilst for the person talking with passion it can be energizing to share their story. Get curious. Find out what their passions are, what inspires them, and what their dreams are. Weave this into the conversations smoothly without jumping around too much. As Dale Carnegie, the famous author of the classic book, How to win friends and influence people said "You can make more friends in two months by becoming interested in other people than you can in two years by trying to get other people interested in you." (Carnegie, 1963)

Show genuine interest in what they are doing. Observe what they are passionate about. This will truly get them talking. Keep things friendly and positive. Ask them about themselves. What are they passionate about? How do they like to spend their free time? Who is their favorite band? What's their favorite movie? Where do they love to travel to? Find out their passions and dive deep. We can be energized by others' enthusiasm and by sharing with you. It drives deep connections between people.

Explore commonalities. Get in tune with them. Conversations can flourish when we have rapport which comes from connecting on the things which we have in common. We tend to warm up to people who we like, and it is easy to connect with people whom we share common ground with. Is there something about them that you potentially have in common? Maybe it's in the way they dress. Maybe it's in their accent. Maybe it's in their attitude. Work on finding and establishing that common ground. If you struggle to find that then work on common ground in your shared environment. For example, comment on the weather or current events. Remember to always frame things in a positive light.

Ask open and closed questions. When asking open questions, it will present you as being interested and engaged. It will also allow the conversation to go deeper without being stopped by a closed answer. Here are some good examples of questions you may ask:

- What do you enjoy doing in your free time?
- What are you passionate about?
- How did you find out about this event?
- How do you know this person?
- Who inspires you?

We all like to be around people that are positive and optimistic. Be the one who is noticing all the good things and shares them with people. Mention interesting things about your surroundings. It could be something as simple as the weather great or this restaurant is super good. On the other hand, if it sucks you could make a joke and flip it to another location. For example, the weather sucks it's one of those days we all wish we were at the beach. Or too bad about the service here, have you tried out the other restaurant? These will open conversations naturally and with ease. You can also praise people for doing a great job. Praise that waiter.

Praise your colleague. Praise your new friend. Be thoughtful and sincere with your praise. Make it a point to find things to compliment people on. Giving someone a compliment can put some sunshine onto their day and make them feel great. It doesn't necessarily have to be about their appearance. Find something you like about them and mention why you like it. It can be anything from their intellect to their previous experiences. Beautiful people say something nonvisual since they probably get compliments on their looks all the time. Maybe you could mention that they come across as being very intelligent. When they ask you why you can take things deeper and add meaning. People love praise and when it's authentic they will warm to you. When giving compliments, always be sincere because people might ask you for more details. Sincerity always shines through.

Remember names

When someone remembers our name, it forges a stronger connection. After all, everyone loves the sound of their own name and there is nothing worse than having to continually repeat it to someone who forgets. Want to know an easy way to remember someone's name? First, say it loud once they say it to you. So, for example, it would go like this. By saying their name out loud it solidifies it into your memory. In addition to really cementing it into your mind repeat it over in your mind five times. Also, imagine any image which you associate with that name. Make use of the first thing that comes to mind. For example, for David, I would think of Dave the rave. Then I would imagine David dancing at a rave. I know it's funny, right? Well, the funnier and weirder the association is the more likely you will be to remember it. Some people suggest adding something sexual there. That's up to you. Do whatever works!

Once you have their name installed in your mind, use it as much as possible when you interact with them. After all, that's their favorite word! Talking to someone using their name instead of a generic pronoun lets them know you at least remember their name, and this helps to form a deeper bond with them.

Empathy

Empathy is an excellent method of building long-lasting connections with people. According to the Merriam-Webster dictionary, empathy is "the action of understanding, being aware of, being sensitive to, and vicariously experiencing the feelings, thoughts, and experience of another" (Merriam-Webster, 2022)

Imagine a great listener who is there for you anytime to listen. You probably feel good being around them. Because they listen without judgment. Sometimes we don't need advice, just someone to talk to. Those with empathy are great at listening. They end up being likable people because it feels like they truly care without having any agenda. Naturally, we want to be around these people.

How can you have more empathy? First of all,

listen more. It really is as simple as that. Sit back and really listen to the other person the next time you have a conversation. Instead of trying to always put your point across, let them have their point. Keep asking questions to go deeper and understand the people you interact with. The more you listen the greater you can become at it. Really tune into what people are saying both with their body language and the words they use.

Talking to groups

Now if you come across groups there is a different style of communication. Extroverts will have a natural advantage when talking to groups. For those of us who are more introverted, shy, or reserved it can be much more difficult. However, by stepping out of your comfort zone it can become possible for you to improve at speaking to groups. After all, if we exclude ourselves from group conversations then it can limit our social life.

One of the most common reasons for people to hold back in group conversations is because of certain unwritten rules which have been engrained and socialized into us. Ultimately, they hold us back. Here are some to be aware of.

- Don't interrupt.
- Don't talk too much about yourself.
- Don't disagree.
- Keep your emotions to yourself.

Imagine how this limits you in group situations. When feeling such feelings, we tend to hold back because we fear being wrong, criticized, or embarrassed. Ultimately, we end up not knowing how or where to fit in. Again, though we can learn and unlearn some of these habits which limit our potential in group conversations.

When you first encounter a group conversation make sure you greet them. Even if you arrived late greet them. If they are already engaged in discussion then a simple nod, smile or saying hello will suffice. Greeting the group will establish your presence with them. Try to engage with them as early as possible. The longer you leave it the more anxiety will build and the further your distance will be from them. The point is to speak up early and loudly enough for everyone to hear.

In addition to speaking up its just as important to be an engaged listener. Give your full attention to whoever is speaking. Pay attention through eye contact, smiling, nodding, and repeating what they say if necessary. Paying more attention to others will not only take the stress off you it will also help you to read the situation. This will help you to understand when to speak. To make your interruptions smoother use body language such as a gesture to let the speaker know that you have a point to make.

Build on current topics instead of switching things early on. By building on current topics, it gets you in the lane of the groups minds and builds rapport with them. Explore the things you agree on. Bond with on similarities which will help you to relate and connect with others in the group. Everyone has their own opinions and ideas. Let them speak theirs and explore together. Be respectful if yours are different. If people show discomfort around certain subjects, then steer away from those subjects. Learn to read the social cues which convey discomfort. For example, when people go quiet, look away or when the conversation dries up. Yes, you should be true to yourself and state your opinions but you don't need to do it in a way that polarizes other people. Furthermore, you don't need to talk about polarizing subjects.

Stay enthusiastic and engaged with the group. Project yourself confidently. Positive energy is attractive. When you speak do so with passion and enthusiasm. That's contagious and will leave a lasting impression on them. Ultimately the best way to get better at talking to groups is through regular practice. The more group conversations you can have the more confident you can become at it. Keep going out there and getting into group conversations. Practice the art.

Story telling

We can tell stories to connect with others more personally, to reveal character traits and to tell personal anecdotes from our lives. But all too often people ramble their way through a story. As such people are not captivated; their attention is lost and the story ends up forgotten. Fortunately, there are more effectives way to tell stories.

Hook

You might think the best place to start a story is at the beginning. Well actually its not. If you want to ensure your story is well received, then first you need to grab your audience's attention. Hook them in by showing them why your story is important. A little highlight is a good start. For instance, you could say something like, "you'll never guess what happened to me last summer". Or "let me tell you about this time we ended up in the most random and scary situation". Essentially you take a highlight of the story and turn it into a compelling headline. The more weird, scary, or emotional it is the more intriguing it will be and the better it will be at gaining the listeners attention.

Ultimately you want your hooks to leave people wanting to hear more. Now if you struggle with this, then simply using words such as weird or funny are good starters. For example, "let me tell you about the 'weird' way I met my husband." When seeding your story don't embellish it too much. Make sure it relates to the content. You don't want to be like a newspaper selling stories with click bait titles.

Imagination

The best stories capture imagination, and you can influence this by inviting your audience to participate. When talking about a pivotal moment in the story ask them what they would do. Or maybe you can ask them what you think happened next and so on. Make sure the questions are open ended. This not only engages their imagination it also locks them into the story and the journey itself.

Paint pictures in their minds. When you tell a story you should take the listener on an emotional journey. Just like they do in the greatest of fiction books use color, smell, texture, sound, and imagery to describe feelings or scenarios. In doing so it will be easier for them to imagine the scene and be connected to you. People will often forget names and words but feelings they rarely forget. Furthermore, describe the emotions you felt. This will help others relate and stay engaged. Engage, engage, engage. Narrate the story well. Your voice is a powerful tool. Avoid being monotone. Vary your tone, speed, and amplitude. Make eye contact with your audience. If you're talking to a group, then mix up eye contact with the participants. Use the information about body language in this book to help you.

Keeping in touch

When we connect well with someone it is a good

idea to keep in touch with them. There are several ways to smoothly do this. Maybe you could ask for their business card, email, or number. Otherwise, social media such as Facebook and Instagram are great ways of keeping in contact whilst also engaging with someone's life. I know it can feel weird to ask someone for their contact information. Maybe it feels like they are thinking you are hitting on them or that you want something from them. Forgot all that. Just be direct and clear that you enjoyed hanging out with them.

During your conversation, you should be exploring mutual interests and reasons to keep in touch. This will make things much smoother when you ask for their contact. For example, I always explore people's interests, hobbies and so on during a conversation. Maybe they like to play pool or are an avid football fan. If you happen to share those interests, then go for it. It will be completely natural for you to hang out with them again as friends. Otherwise just say something like "hey it was great meeting you if you want to hang out sometime hit me up". "Do you use WhatsApp, Instagram, or something else?"

Once you have someone's contact information ping them right away so that you are in their inbox. Restate what you talked about during your interaction. For example, "hey let's play pool sometime". "Or let me know where a good place is to watch the game." Don't worry if they are flakey. Personally, I would avoid this kind of person anyway. Remember most people know up to one hundred and fifty people. That circle of friends narrows down to closer relationships. Maybe they make it through, or maybe they don't. Realistically everyone has their own commitments, lifestyles and so on. Keep meeting new people and trying to connect with them. After all it's a numbers game.

When we start building new groups of friends it's going to feel awesome. But I want to highlight one super, super important aspect here. Responsibility. Write that down and install it into your mind. Responsibility is on you. If your home alone each night, then that is on you. You need to be the one calling up your friends. You need to be the one setting up the plans. Don't take it personally when no one calls you. People have their own agenda and will do their own thing most of the time. But if you reach out to offer them an interesting and easy option then you will have a packed social life. Don't doubt yourself and think they might reject you. No instead set up an easy plan, in advance such as having drinks at a reasonable time at an accessible place. Imagine you are going anyway and you're just inviting them along.

One of my close friends seems to know everyone and always has plans for the weekend. So how does he do it? Well one thing I noticed which he is very good at and finds useful is being in various chat groups. He will create a chat group for an upcoming event. Say for example a BBQ or just for friends in a certain city which makes it easy to be in contact with a group of friends all at the same time. After all we usually get lazy and just text our closest friends to go out. The line ends there. Why not reach more friends in a group? Plus people will then start posting activities or meetups that you could join.

Another thing my well-connected friend does is to call you. These days calling someone is unheard of. People text, dm and so on which is very non personal because for example we don't hear their voice. True you can leave voice notes which is a step further but you're not having a real, live conversation. A quick call sticks in your mind and brings you closer in communication. Plus, you get a quicker response. This friend and I weren't that close before, but he is often the first one I would call if going out. Try it for yourself. Make a quick phone call just to see how your friends are doing. If they don't pick up, leave a voice note.

One last useful tool is your calendar. Google calendar is the best because it will sync across your devices. Use it to schedule in all your social appointments. The simple act of planning and scheduling your social life will fit it up more. You can even color code the various events. Maybe the colors are for events, meeting with friends, dates and so on. Go ahead and fill up that calendar!

SOCIAL SKILLS & STICKING POINTS

Realize that none of us are perfect at socializing. We all have our own individual social flaws and drawbacks. Indeed, now, and then you may well suffer sticking points in your social life to some degree. Imagine carving out a rock to get to the gold in the middle. The external rock is all that shyness, weird ticks, lack of confidence and so on. The gold in the middle is your social freedom to be yourself. Indeed, you will have to be vulnerable to show that. But that is true strength.

We all love to be around people who are real.

Those people show vulnerability. Just think of your favorite movies. The actors were very good at being vulnerable and they they their gold shine through. You too must share your gold with the world because in revealing this your relationships with people will improve as they see your true nature. True it might alienate some people but that's just being real. Please remember that you should never be rude or offensive. Always be a kind and polite person. The inherent truth is some people will vibe with you and some won't. Your goal should be to build a tribe your vibe with. Let's work on getting to your gold.

Social awkwardness

Do you ever find yourself lost for words? Do you often say the wrong thing or jumble up your words? Well, if you answered yes to any of those questions then you are probably suffering from being socially awkward. Realize that it doesn't define you. Simply it's just a fleeting feeling that you can eventually overcome. In fact, all of us suffer from being socially awkward from time to time.

So, what exactly is social awkwardness? Essentially it is the perception that you have made a mistake or feeling like you have done something wrong. For example, you feel like you don't fit in with the group. Or you worry about your shirt being too small. Or you tripped over in front of people. These transgressions affect your behavior and manifest as social awkwardness. Specifically, those behaviors are anxiety, avoidance, and hesitation.

Now that you fully understand and are aware of social awkwardness you can work on overcoming it. First be present with any discomfort you might be experiencing. Realize that it will come and eventually go. Otherwise, it can be a vicious cycle of feeling even more awkward because your drawing attention to your awkwardness. So just be aware of it and accept it. When you worry and overthink about if you're saying or doing the right thing it can make you appear insincere and strategic. Other people will pick up on that vibe which you give off. This can make it hard for them to trust you because you're coming off as inauthentic. It's like you're hiding something. If you're feeling a little nervous or tired. Own it and share it. Make light of it or even make a joke about it. "Oh, here it comes again. Sorry guys I know I'm being awkward, but I haven't been out of my cave for a while". Vulnerability is strength and being open about it is warming to others. Authenticity means that you know what your strengths and weaknesses are. You're able to deal with them in a considerate way. People will be much more understanding and receptive then you think. Focus on the other people you are engaging with to direct the focus away from you. This will help to calm down any awkwardness.

One last thing you need to aware of is perfectionism. Many people who suffer from social awkwardness have a desire to be perfect. They want to look their best, to speak their best and to act their best. But life isn't like that. People perceive you subjectively. Some people might think you're a fool whilst others will love you. Reasons why they might think such things cannot be explained. Learn to be ok with all of that and learn to let go of trying to be perfect or trying to please everyone. Be yourself. Now don't be a lazy bum without making any effort. Of course, always do your best but don't attach yourself to being perfect. We as humans enjoy the story and arc of a character. Flaws and transgressions make us more human. Be ok with making mistakes. Stop micro-analyzing your behavior and how you are perceived. Stop overthinking the situation. Let it all go and stop filtering who you are. Just be yourself and embrace the awkwardness!

Social anxiety disorder

According to research from the National Institute of Mental Health, almost seven percent of Americans are estimated to have experienced social anxiety during the last year. (Social

Anxiety Disorder, 2022) For women, it is twice as likely as for men. Current research indicates that a small part of the brain called the amygdala is believed to be where fear responses come from. Those with relatives suffering from it are more likely to inherit it. In addition, the environment plays a huge influence. Childhood maltreatment and adversity are big influences on social anxiety disorder.

Social anxiety disorder or otherwise known as social phobia is a feeling of overwhelming anxiety and self-consciousness. Certain situations can elevate those feelings. For example, public speaking or just being around new people. Those suffering from it tend to feel an intense and persistent fear of being judged. They feel like they are being watched by others and worry about being embarrassed or humiliated. Simple daily life can become problematic for them. Left untreated it can become a major hindrance to life and often leads to low self-esteem and depression.

Furthermore, many people seek to pacify their negative feelings through drugs and alcohol abuse which can lead to addiction.

In addition to the mental symptoms of social anxiety disorder there are associated physical symptoms. Those include shaking, nausea, sweating, blushing and difficulty speaking. Because these symptoms are visible, they can further heighten the mental symptoms which ends up in an increasing, vicious cycle. Other symptoms include avoiding social situations. For example, people suffering social anxiety disorder might avoid simple things such as, telephone calls, public speaking, meeting new people, figures of authority and crowded places.

Social anxiety disorder can be treated with great success by a trained mental healthcare professional. Treatment consists of psychotherapy and medications. Cognitive-behavioral therapy (CBT) is a style of psychotherapy that can be highly effective at treating the disorder. (Weekes, 1990) The process involves reducing anxiety by eliminating behaviors and beliefs that support the anxiety disorder. Essentially one would be encouraged to define and imagine their worst fears. By getting to understand their fears more closely they can then learn how to deal with them. Through time and proper practice with a trained therapist one can gradually reduce their social anxiety disorder.

Dealing with nerves

I know you will probably feel a lot of nervous energy around talking to strangers and starting conversations. Sometimes our brains work against us and in those times, it certainly isn't helping us to make new friends. When in new social situations it can be difficult to get comfortable because it's overwhelming us. Particularly with strangers or in new environments comfort can be cumbersome to attain. What we need to do is assume comfort and command our brain to assume we feel that we already know the people we are about to meet. Let your brain know who is in control. This gives us a good start which increases our positive first impression and the chances of people liking us. The next time you meet new people. Assume you know them already. Practice liking things about the people you come across. Imagine they are your friends and how well you are all connected. People will always remember you for how you made them feel.

Learn to control and calm your nerves and anxieties which are essentially trapped energy in the body. Settling your body down can help to calm this energy. As a newbie you will probably be shaking and nervous at the thought of socializing. Simply shake that energy out. Go somewhere private such as a restroom stool. I regularly used this hack before big shows when I was a DJ. Essentially, you are shaking the nervous energy out. Begin by jumping up and down. Keep your body straight like a pogo stick jumping style and let the impact go out through your feet. Jump up and down ten to twenty times.

Next, stand up straight with your back slightly leaning back. Extend your arms over your head and back to your shoulders. Imagine you're reaching for some apples with both arms. As you reach exhale. As you pull back, inhale. Repeat this quickly for ten to twenty times. Next beach your chest like a gorilla ten to twenty times. Feeling less anxious? Great, do another two to three rounds of this until you feel looser. If you're going to be talking a lot, then warm up your voice also. You can hum a low note and pitch it up. Go up and down. Combine this with vowel sounds and lip trills to warm the voice up. All of this makes a huge difference on having a clear voice. Remember to do this in private if you can because it will look weird. But trust me it helps!

For very anxious people it can be useful to try some affirmations. Write down twenty present tense statements of a character trait you wish you have. The concept is that by saying these out loud it programs your subconscious to be in alignment with these beliefs. There is nothing proven with these, but they are subjective and therefore might work for you. Again, if you're a newbie or have social anxiety then go ahead and with anything that can help you. For example:

- I am confident
- I am charismatic
- I am social and outgoing

Shyness

People who suffer from shyness will feel awkward or apprehensive when being approached or when approaching others. On a biological level they are responding to a fear which is created through life experiences and parenting. Since shyness stems from excessive self-conscious it proves that people aren't born shy because consciousness develops in early childhood. Later in adolescence it can and often does progresses.

Symptoms of shyness emerge when a person

becomes overly self-conscious. Often, they will make unrealistic comparisons of themselves against more outgoing people. Social skills become difficult and as such they will often avoid social situations. Not too be confused with introversion shyness is quite different. Introverts are energized through spending time alone whilst shy people often want to connect with others but don't know how to.

Overcoming shyness will require you to step outside of your comfort zone. But it can be made easier by preparing for social events in advance. This will help to reduce any self-consciousness and anxieties. Plan out a few talking points and questions to ask in advance. Take on the mindset that you are already confident and outgoing. Instead of dwelling on what might not go right instead focus on what could go right. Keep practicing by attending more social events and engaging with the people you come across. Shyness isn't going away on its own. Continual practice and exposure will help you.

Emotions

Emotions influence our behaviors and thoughts. In turn, they shape our social and professional lives. Recent research by (Parkinson, 1996; Van Kleef, 2009) has discovered that emotions are inherently social meaning that they are expressed and elicited towards and from others. Furthermore, they are regulated to comply with social customs. A growing body of research has demonstrated the social influences on shaping emotions. Essentially, they are a key component of our social lives. When people experience emotions, they often share them with others. The sharing of emotions proves that they are invariably social in nature. (Kleef, 2016)

Emotions can be expressed through body movements, expressions and through the face. For example, when someone is angry or happy it is easy to see in their expressions Emotions are essentially psychological states consisting of feelings, thoughts, physiological changes, inclinations, and expressions. The combinations of these elements determine the emotions and behaviors they elicit. An event both real or experienced is what triggers these complex states and behaviors. Perhaps someone compliments or insults you. The nature of the event and your perception of it will determine the emotions you end up feeling. Maybe you get angry, happy, or annoyed. These states can cause physiological changes in your body such as face reddening, body tension and so on. This may cause you to react physically or verbally. In hindsight you might recall the original emotion and in turn feel gratitude or remorse depending on the context.

Emotions will cause us to sometimes not feel like going out or being social. Maybe you just want to chill and do your own thing. I know how that feels. Or you're out with friends and you just aren't feeling it. You're in your head. In those times it's good to just cut the time down or take a break from it. We can all get burned out from too much socializing. Especially if you're an introvert then it can be quite tiring. Allow yourself some time to recalibrate and recover. Get a good night's sleep and do some things you enjoy which are recharging you. That could be going swimming, watching some podcasts, or having a long sleep. After that you should be good to go back out.

We all get moody from time to time. There will be days when you feel on the top of the world whilst some days you want to hide all day under the covers. It's all normal. We are all humans and not robots. A mood is part of our emotional rhythms. They tend to be less intense than emotions and usually are the result of events or experiences. They can be brief or hang around for a while. Perhaps you had an argument and it put you in a bad mood. Or you went to a seminar, and it put you in an upbeat mood. Most moods will pass in a day.

To determine our behaviors and causes we need to dive in and understand our moods. Feeling good when in a positive mood is understandable as is feeling bad in a negative mood. When we begin to explore our moods, it can be useful indicators of things that need to be addressed. Maybe it's a work-life balance. Or biological changes. To help you get to the causes, here are some common causes of negative moods.

- Lack of sleep
- Hunger
- Stress
- Interactions with others
- Hormonal changes
- The media
- The weather
- Exercise
- Burn out
- Drugs and alcohol
- Side effects of medications
- Poor nutrition
- Disorders
- Illnesses
- Mental health

- Environment

Monitor your emotions and moods to find out what triggers them. Become more mindful and self-aware which will help you to cultivate a more wholesome lifestyle. The side benefit of this improved life is better social interactions. When we are more upbeat it attracts us to more people giving us more confidence and inspiration. (Emotions - IResearchNet, 2019)

Therapy

If your still stuck and it's becoming a burden, then I suggest you seek professional help. Therapy used to have a fair amount of stigma around it. People tend to think it's only for the really screwed up or crazy people. But did you know that the rich and famous have been gaining tons of value from it for many years? Incidentally with the pandemic being a huge burden on people's mental health it has recently blown up in popularity. There are so many different platforms and services offering therapy online. Unless you can find one to personally visit then go online. Just search Google for online therapists offering free fifteen-minute trials. Test out a bunch of them until you find the one you vibe with and who you think can help you the most.

For a friend of mine, two years of weekly therapy helped her to overcome her natural introversion and become comfortable going to social events without getting burned out. This has had a dramatic and positive impact on her life. Nowadays she regularly attends group meet ups and is someone with a packed social life. Personally, therapy has helped me to understand my past, heal wounds and to explore my darker sides. It sounds weird I know but we are all a little bit messed up in our own ways. Exploring this is going to help you progress as a human being and in turn make you a better friend.

Limiting beliefs and journaling

We have our conscious mind and our subconscious mind. Our conscious mind is what we are aware of. We make conscious decisions such as what to eat, where to go, what to do and so on. Underneath that is our subconscious mind which makes a ton of other decisions. According to scientific research the subconscious mind is what makes most decisions. Meanwhile our conscious mind makes just a few. Your subconscious is like an autopilot system with a ton of information based on your biology, experiences, and beliefs. It uses these to make those decisions which influence and dictate the path of your life. Many of those decisions might be hurting you and as such they need to be brought into the light and reframed. These are limiting beliefs. Essentially, they are beliefs which limit our potential. Outlined below is a system for reframing them.

1. Capture – for the next week write down anytime you experience some negative kind of emotion which you feel is holding you back.

    a. Capture that into a statement.

For example, you see someone you want to talk to, but you don't. Maybe it's - I am not good enough.

2. Explore – at the end of the week start to explore those statements. For example – I am not good enough.

    a. Dive deeper into it.

      i. Where does this belief come from?

        1. I am not good enough to talk to this person.

      ii. Why?

        1. Because I am not successful enough.

      iii. Can I be more specific?

        1. Because I haven't made it in life yet.

3. Reframe – in this step we explore the truth and reality in those statements and answers from exploration. We want to make this not believable anymore. Ask the questions such as.

Is this really true? Try to find evidence.

   a. I am not good enough to talk to this person – is this really true? – well to be honest there is no law against talking to another person. I should probably just go for it.

   b. Because I am not successful enough – how do I know that? Do you know the life history of this person? I don't think so.

   c. Because I haven't made it in life yet – who has? What is the definition of that? Aren't we all on our own journeys? This doesn't stop me from talking to someone.

4. Empower – now that we have disproven those incorrect beliefs, we no longer need to believe in them. Therefore, it makes sense for us to reframe them into something more

empowering. Let's look at our examples.

a. I am not good enough to talk to this person – I am confident enough to talk to anyone.

b. I am not successful enough – I am more than enough, right here, right now.

c. I haven't made it in life yet – I am proud of myself and believe in myself.

Make this exercise a regular activity. Go a step further and create images for it if you can. Find images you associate with the new beliefs. For example, images of superman, of a successful person or a social person or a lion. You get the idea. Keep it on your phone, print it out or keep it where you will look at it often.

PERSONALITY

—ℓℓ—

Personality is a detailed and useful subject when it comes to making friends and becoming better at socializing. Understanding it will help you to evaluate the people who could become your friends. What's the point of all this? When we can understand personality and how it is quantified it can help us to understand people better along with their individual differences. This can give us a better understanding of how to articulate and communicate ideas to them which is great in social or professional environments. For example, knowing what kind of situations to invite certain friends to. Or in a workplace knowing who to a project delegate to. Furthermore, it influences mental health. Therefore, it is a great tool to understand yourself.

Essentially personality is the distinctive patterns of behavior, thoughts, and feelings of a particular person. These can change over one's lifetime. However certain traits tend to remain consistent into adulthood. So why do we have the personalities we have? Do they change over time? First of all, genetics play a huge role. Next the roles we take on can influence our personality significantly. Roles such as being a sibling, a spouse, or a parent. Generally, it stays stable throughout a lifetime and as we mature, we gain more social sensitivity. As such we naturally adjust certain traits such as agreeableness and openness. Furthermore, through repeated effort we can make changes. For example, working with a therapist can help you with exposure if your rating is high in neuroticism.

Each person has a combination of an infinite number of characteristics that are beyond the scope of standard personality terminology. However, a general standard exists, and this is something that has been studied since ancient Greek times. Nowadays psychologists have summarized personality into the big five traits. Those are as follows, openness, conscientiousness, extraversion, agreeableness, and neuroticism. In addition, there is a newer model known as HEXACO which adds honesty-humility as a sixth key trait. (Lee & Ashton, 2012)

Whilst there are other studies and quantifications of personality type such as a "Type A" personality or the types supplied by the popular Myers-Briggs Type Indicator (MBTI). (Myers & Myers, 1995). These have been challenged by scientists and psychologists who study personality as being too simplistic in their analysis. Alternatively, they suggest that frameworks such as the Big Five model provides a more accurate assessment. When analyzing someone's personality using the Big Five model, they can be placed somewhere on a continuum for each of the traits. In comparison to others, they might be rated relatively high or low on a trait. It is the combination of these varying trait levels which determines someone's unique personality.

To assess a person's individual traits there are several different personality tests that can be applied. Typically, these tests assess the extent to which a variety of descriptions of thoughts and behaviors reflect their own uniqueness. Responses determine the rating of a particular measure on a trait. When analyzing the traits realize that there is nothing wrong with being at any end of each scale. They are neither bad nor good. It is merely someone's personality. Often you won't be totally on one side of a scale or the other. Personality isn't as black and white as that. Rather it's more shades and most of us will fall somewhere in the middle on most traits. Again, remember none of it is neither good nor bad. So be honest with yourself and get attain an accurate reading. (Kazdin, 2000) (Personality, 2022)

Openness

Openness also known as openness to experience and open mindedness. Essentially it is how open a person is to new ideas or experiences. Individuals high in openness are curious and creative. Are you open to new ideas? Do you like to visit new places? Or do you prefer the predictable? Where would you rate yourself on the scale of openness?

Conscientiousness

Conscientiousness is essentially how a person deals with impulses in order to be more responsible and productive. This can be reflected in how organized, disciplined, and productive they are. Individuals high in conscientiousness are determined and persistent in their pursuit towards a goal. Do you get distracted easily? Do you have many regrets? Are you organized? Where would you rate yourself on the scale of conscientiousness?

Extroversion

Extroversion is essentially the level of energy with which a person engages with the world and other people. Individuals high in extroversion are typically very social, outgoing, and assertive. The opposite of extroversion is introversion where a person is more internally focused. Are you energized by big social events? Do you meet new people easily? Or do you prefer a quiet night at home? Where would you rate yourself on the scale of extroversion?

Agreeableness

Agreeableness is essentially a person's amount of helpfulness, willingness, and positivity towards other people. Individuals high in agreeableness are polite and respectful towards others. They also tend to be altruists and trust others. Are you involved with any charity? Are you a good listener? Are you always going along with the plan of your friends? Do you trust people easily? Where would you rate yourself on the scale of agreeableness?

Neuroticism

Neuroticism is essentially a person's disposition to experiencing challenging emotions such as depression, anxiety, or negative emotions. Highly neurotic people will often be more easily influenced to feel negative emotions and are less emotionally stable. Do you get angry or nervous easily? Do you suffer from social anxiety? Do you worry or overthink? Where would you rate yourself on the scale of neuroticism?

HEXACO, Honesty-Humility

The added sixth major personality trait is Honesty-Humility. Essentially this is the degree to which one places themselves ahead of others. For example, by manipulation or through seeking special treatment. Proposed facets include being humble, fair, sincere, and avoiding greed. Do you brag about your achievements? Do you post on social media often? Or do you work in silence and let your results speak for you? Where would you rate yourself on the scale of Honesty-Humility?

Introversion and extroversion

Introversion is a type of personality that is personified by one's preference to their inner mind over the external world of people. It is on the opposite spectrum of extroversion which one prefers the external world of people. Introverts prefer to have a more chilled out and solitary experience or to be with smaller more intimate groups. Extroverts on the other hand prefer large groups and like being at the center of attention.

Introverts aren't antisocial, it's just that they tend to draw energy from having their alone time. Indeed, they are likely to enjoy being with groups of friends but for too long it can tire them. One to one interactions and calmer environments are preferable for them. Extroverts on the other hand tend to thrive in big group events. Usually, they can go all night at social gatherings without their energy dropping too much. It's important to note here that most people are not one hundred percent introverted or extroverted. It isn't as black and white as that. Most people are somewhere between the two, maybe leaning more towards one side than the other. Those who display both are defined ambiverts. In addition, all people will at some point need to recharge their energy.

Identifying if someone is an introvert or extrovert can help you significantly in your relationships. It will help you to understand their communication style and what kinds of interests they are likely to have. Introverts can be identified as being quieter at social events with group settings. They will probably be the first to leave a party. Extroverts are easier to spot. They will be more expressive, louder, and energetic at social gatherings.

The Dark Triad of personality

Beware things are about to get dark right now! Following on here are three personality traits which you will need to be aware of. These traits are known as the dark triad which are as follows, narcissism, psychopathy, and Machiavellianism. Essentially, they are used as a way of investigating and assessing the darker side of human psychology. Again, just like the big five traits they are a scale on which most people are not fully at one or the other side. Furthermore, we all might have a little bit of a dark triad inside of us and it can come out at various times in our lives. Realize that it's something to be aware of in ourselves and in the people whom we socialize with. Although as mentioned a person can rate high, low, or in between. Be open minded in your assessments here.

(Lockard & Paulhus, 1988)

Narcissism

Narcissism is essentially a person's sense of entitlement and self-importance towards others. Those high in narcissism are often attention seekers who have an excessive need for being admired. Do you crave attention? Do you enjoy people giving you praise? Do you like the sound of your own voice a little too much? Where would you rate yourself on the scale of neuroticism?

Psychopathy

Psychopathy is essentially a person who lacks any sense of empathy, remorse or has trouble controlling impulses. Such a person should be handled with caution because they tend to hurt others mentally and physically without remorse. Do you enjoy seeing others worse off than you? Are you impulsive? Or do you celebrate the wins of others? Where would you rate yourself on the scale of psychopathy?

Machiavellianism

Machiavellianism is essentially a person who tends to manipulate others to gain an advantage. This is named after Niccolò Machiavelli, the 16th-century author of the famous book on strategy, The Prince. Are you manipulative? Are you friends with people because you like them? Or are your relationships only for gain? Where would you rate yourself on the scale of Machiavellianism? (Machiavelli, 1984)

CONCLUSION

In the introduction of this book, I presented a system to you. Now you can apply that system to your life. Whether you want to make a new best friend, gain a new social circle or even to find a relationship it will help you. I promise you once again here that you too can have a fulfilling social life. Out there is there is a world full of people waiting to meet you. People who could be your friends and whom you could share your life with.

Early on in this book I told you that the most important part of it is the section about metrics. Remember that I told you to create a spreadsheet and record the number of people you speak to each week? If you commit to that and aim to talk to at least twenty to thirty people a week, then you're going to see significant results in your social life. Recording the data will motivate you to act and will encourage better results. Sometimes all you need to do is to say "hi" or "how you". After all, seemingly small conversations can lead to new friendships and much more.

Keep reviewing your progress each week. The amount of people you talked to. How it went. What you need to improve. Actions you need to take and so on. Incidentally why not take it a step further and seek out feedback from other people? A fresh set of eyes can help to identify any blind spots you might have. Ask a friend who you can rely on for their authentic and constructive feedback. Otherwise consider hiring a social skills coach to come out with you occasionally. Let them know you want feedback and specific things to work on improving.

Taking metrics and notes will feed whatever your social life goals happen to be. Realize that it's important for you have goals. Early on in this book I presented you some questions which will help you to identify whatever it is you want. Those goals should be clearly written down. Make use of all the tools and tips and methods in this book to achieve them.

I encourage you to revisit parts of this book whenever you happen to get stuck. From how to meet new people, to connecting with them and build lasting friendships. All of this has been covered in depth. Keep working on all the parts, making good first impressions, having great conversations, overcoming your social weaknesses and so on. The knowledge in this book is just the tip of the iceberg. Keep an open mind to new knowledge. Soak up other ideas from similar books in addition to studying courses and videos. Udemy has many quality and affordable courses whilst YouTube has tons of amazing free content within this niche. On both platforms you can find so much great content on areas such as, body language tutorials or real-world examples of socializing. Seminars are great too. Not only will you meet a bunch of like-minded individuals who could turn into new friends you will also be learning. There are thousands of seminars, just look around your region or further afield for the best ones. Remember to put into practice whatever you learn and be willing to try it out.

Life can be tough and it's not fun to be alone all the time. Whatever our circumstances are, we must always try to stay connected with friends and be social. It's fun to share memories and experiences with friends. It's fun to meet new people. Everything you want in life is going to come through connection. The only thing that holds you back is you. The moment you can connect with someone it can last forever. Stop holding back, take responsibility, take action and make it happen. Step out into the world, challenge your comfort zone, and start meeting new people. Sometimes you will have to go out alone. Just be brave and be bold. Yes, there will be times when it feels weird and difficult, but progress is all about that. This is a journey and one that you should enjoy.

Embrace the ride.

REFERENCES

Carnegie, D. (1963). How to Win Friends & Influence People (Revised ed.). Pocket Books.

Charisma (2022). Psychology Today. https://www.psychologytoday.com/us/basi cs/charisma

Confidence. (2022). Psychology Today. https://www.psychologytoday.com/us/basi cs/confidence

Dunbar, R. (2010). How Many Friends Does One Person Need? Dunbar's Number and Other Evolutionary Quirks (Main ed.). Faber & Faber.

Emotions - IResearchNet. (2019, November 12). Psychology. http://psychology.iresearchnet.com/social-psychology/emotions/

How to Make a Good First Impression: Expert Tips and Tricks. (2022). Betterup. https://www.betterup.com/blog/how-to-make-a-good-first-impression

Kazdin, A. E. (2000). Encyclopedia of

Psychology: 8-Volume Set 8-Volume Set (1st ed.). American Psychological Association.

Kleef, G. V. A. (2016). Editorial: The Social Nature of Emotions. Frontiers. https://www.frontiersin.org/articles/10.33 89/fpsyg.2016.00896/full

Lee, K., & Ashton, M. C. (2012). The H Factor of Personality: Why Some People are Manipulative, Self-Entitled, Materialistic, and Exploitive—And Why It Matters for Everyone (Illustrated ed.). Wilfrid Laurier University Press.

Lockard, J. S., & Paulhus, D. L. (1988). Self-Deception: An Adaptive Mechanism (Century Psychology Series) (1st ed.). Prentice Hall.

Lowndes, L. (2003). How to Talk to Anyone: 92 Little Tricks for Big Success in Relationships (1st ed.). McGraw Hill.

Machiavelli, N. (1984). Discourses (4.1.1984 ed.). Penguin Classics.

Merriam-Webster. (2022). The Merriam-Webster Dictionary. Merriam-Webster, Incorporated.

Myers, I. B., & Myers, P. B. (1995). Gifts Differing: Understanding Personality Type

(2nd ed.). CPP.

Olson, J. (2013). The Slight Edge (Anniversary ed.). Success Books.

Personality. (2022). APA. https://www.apa.org/topics/personality

Shortsleeve, C. (2018, August 28). How to Make the Best First Impression, According to Experts. Time. https://time.com/5374799/best-first-impression-experts/

Social Anxiety Disorder. (2022). National Institute of Mental Health (NIMH). https://www.nimh.nih.gov/health/statistics/social-anxiety-disorder

Weekes, C. (1990). The Latest Help for Your Nerves. HarperCollins Publishers.

Willis, J., & Todorov, A. (2006). First Impressions. Psychological Science, 17(7), 592–598. https://doi.org/10.1111/j.1467-9280.2006.01750.x

RITUALS OF THE RICH & FAMOUS

Free Success Tips, Strategies, and Habits of the Rich & Famous.

For new strategies every week on how to be more productive, confident, and happy.

JOIN SUCCESSFUL SUBSCRIBERS!

Simply scan the QR code to join.

www.ingramcontent.com/pod-product-compliance
Lightning Source LLC
Chambersburg PA
CBHW050729030426
42336CB00012B/1477